Tiptoe Into Scary Places

SCARY MUSEUMS

by Joyce Markovics

Consultant: Debbie Felton
Professor of Classics
University of Massachusetts
Amherst, Massachusetts

BEARPORT PUBLISHING

Minneapolis, Minnesota

Credits

Cover, © Kim Jones, © Breaking The Walls/Stutterstock, © Nerthuz/Stutterstock, © J.Croese/Stutterstock, and © BOONCHUAY PROMJIAM/Stutterstock; 3, © aswphotos134/Shutterstock; 4-5, © Kim Jones; 6, © Kovtun Dmitriy/Shutterstock and © Phichai/Shutterstock; 7, © Diego Jesus Sanchez Torres/Alamy; 8, © Thiago Santos/Alamy; 9, © Prisma by Dukas Presseagentur GmbH/Alamy; 10, © Artokoloro Quint Lox Limited/Alamy; 11, © Steve Vidler/Alamy; 12T, © Ungar-Biewer/Shutterstock; 12B, © CBN Polona/Wikimedia Commons; 13, © lapas77/Shutterstock; 15, © Tony/Wikimedia Commons; 16, © Linda Harms/Shutterstock; 17, © jalejandro/Shutterstock and © Donna Beeler/Shutterstock; 18, © loyaldefender2004/Wikimedia Commons; 19, © Bob Pardue - Midwest/Alamy; 20, © Fer Gregory/Shutterstock; 21, © Yodchai Prominn/Shutterstock; 23, © Clem Hencher-Stevens/Shutterstock; and 24, © Poring Studio/Shutterstock.

President: Jen Jenson
Director of Product Development: Spencer Brinker
Editor: Allison Juda
Designer: Micah Edel
Cover: Kim Jones

Library of Congress Cataloging-in-Publication Data

Names: Markovics, Joyce L., author.
Title: Scary museums / by Joyce Markovics.
Description: Minneapolis, Minnesota : Bearport Publishing Company, [2021] | Series: Tiptoe into scary places | Includes bibliographical references and index.
Identifiers: LCCN 2020002396 (print) | LCCN 2020002397 (ebook) | ISBN 9781647471767 (library binding) | ISBN 9781647471828 (ebook)
Subjects: LCSH: Haunted museums—Juvenile literature.
Classification: LCC BF1476.5 .M368 2021 (print) | LCC BF1476.5 (ebook) | DDC 133.1/22—dc23
LC record available at https://lccn.loc.gov/2020002396
LC ebook record available at https://lccn.loc.gov/2020002397

For more information, write to Bearport Publishing, 5357 Penn Avenue South, Minneapolis, MN 55419. Printed in the United States of America.

CONTENTS

Scary Museums

Dusty museum shelves are crowded with cobwebs and old objects. Each one holds a secret story. Beware of moving shadows and blasts of cold air. The long-dead owners of these **ancient** items may want them back.

Get ready to read four spine-tingling stories about spooky museums. Turn the page . . . if you dare.

MASSES OF MUMMIES

***Museo de las Momias de Guanajuato*, Guanajuato, Mexico**

Visitors flock to this creepy museum in a graveyard to get a close-up look at dozens of **mummies**!

From around 1870 to 1958, bodies in this Guanajuato (gwah-nah-WAH-toh) graveyard were dug up if the person's loved ones could not afford to pay a fee. Surprisingly, many of the **corpses** had become mummies. They were placed in a nearby building, which later became a museum.

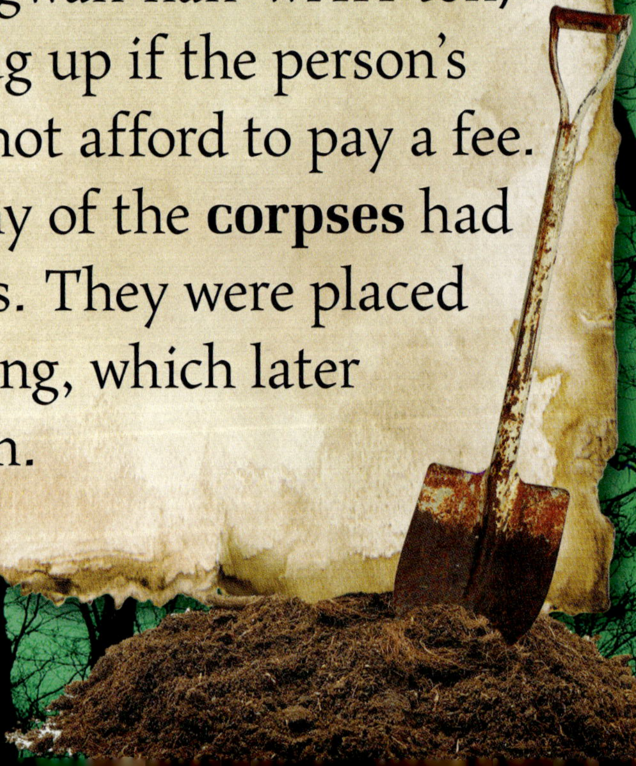

A mummy in Guanajuato

The mummies in the museum come in many spooky shapes and sizes. Some have open mouths and twisted faces as if they're calling out for help. People say becoming a mummy in this museum was **punishment** for people who did bad things while they were alive.

The smallest mummy in the world is found in the museum. It is the body of a tiny baby.

Night Terrors

Victoria and Albert Museum, London, England

The Great Bed of Ware is a giant four-poster bed. It was made around 1590 by a master **craftsman** who covered the bed in beautiful carvings.

Over the years, the bed was used at an inn in Ware, England. Travelers often carved their initials into the bedposts. It's believed that's when the ghostly attacks began.

An illustration of the Bed of Ware

Legend says the ghost of the craftsman protects the bed. If anybody tries to sleep in it, he pinches, pokes, and scratches the person.

Today, the Great Bed of Ware is at the Victoria and Albert Museum in London, England. Many people believe the ghost still haunts the bed.

The bed was so famous that William Shakespeare talked about it in one of his plays!

Victoria and Albert Museum

GHOST HOUSE

Merchant's House Museum, New York, New York

For almost 100 years, members of the Tredwell family lived in a large, brick row house. Many of them *died* there, too, including Gertrude Tredwell. She was the last person to live in the home before it became a museum. Does her **spirit** remain in the place she so dearly loved?

Gertrude Tredwell died in 1933 at the age of 93.

The Merchant's House Museum

Not long after Gertrude's death, a ghostly old lady began appearing in the house. People saw the **phantom** gliding up the stairs and standing in doorways. Visitors have experienced cold bursts of air in one of the rooms—the same room where Gertrude died.

A courtyard behind the Mercant's Museum

LOST SOULS

Glore Psychiatric Museum, St. Joseph, Missouri

For 100 years, this building was an overcrowded hospital for the mentally ill. The treatments there were often harmful—and even deadly. Some **patients** were locked in metal cages or in **coffin**-sized boxes. Others were dunked in ice water. Some of them drowned.

A chair used to torture patients

Glore Psychiatric Museum

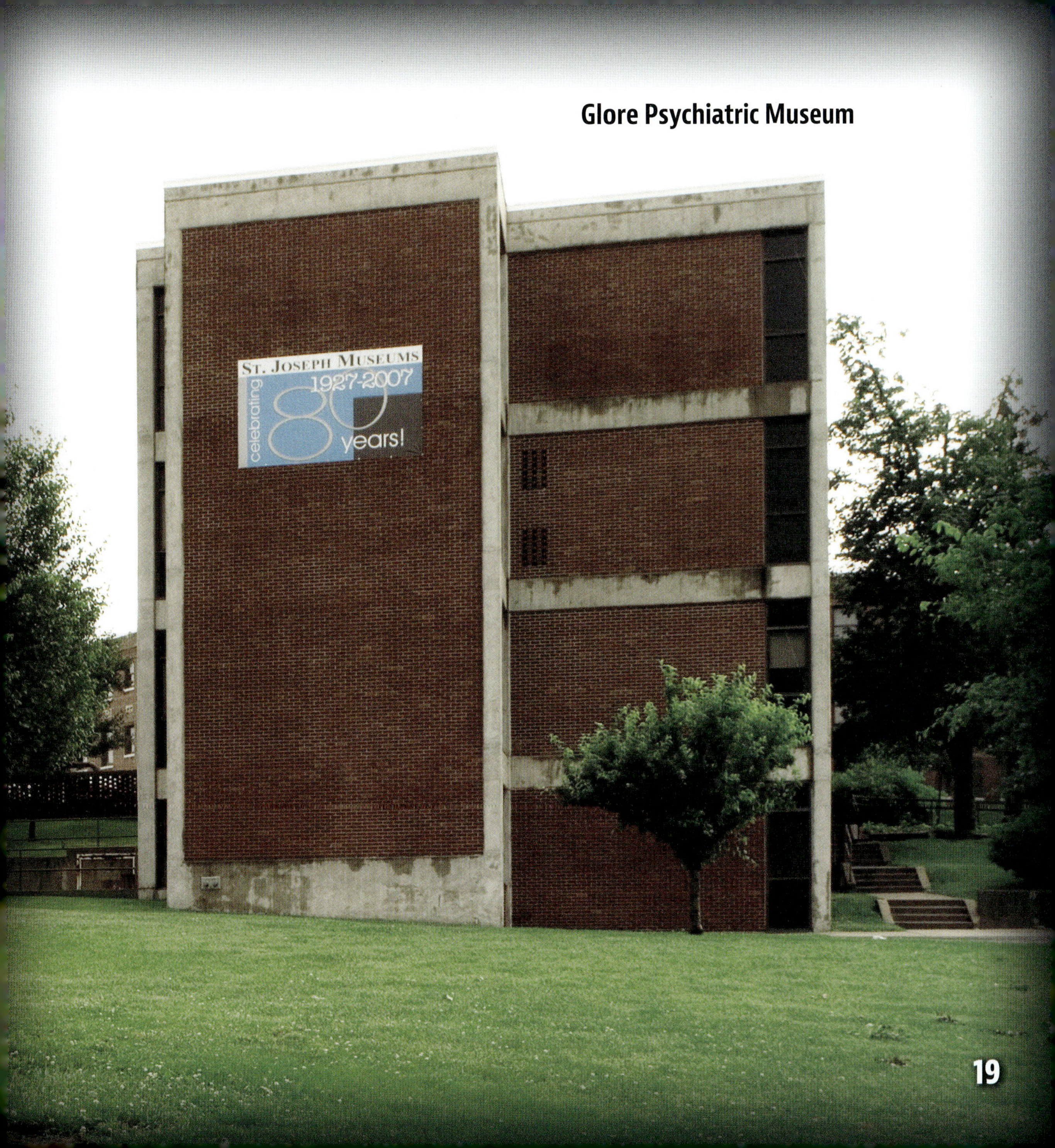

The hospital became the Glore Psychiatric Museum where visitors claim to see a shadowy figure in the basement. It runs down the hall and shouts a warning. A woman's voice has also been heard, whimpering and crying out for help. Are these the ghosts of patients who died trying to get well?

While the hospital was open, more than 2,000 patients died there. The building had its very own **morgue**, which is now part of the museum.

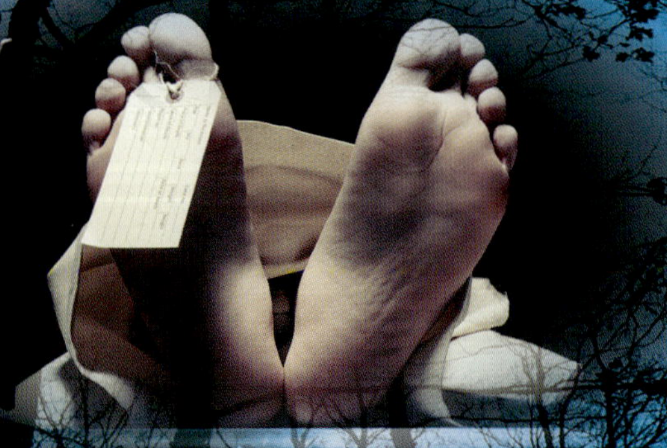

Scary Museums Around the World

Museo de las Momias de Guanajuato
Guanajuato, Mexico

Visit a museum packed with mummies.

Glore Psychiatric Museum
St. Joseph, Missouri

Learn about this museum's dark past from the ghosts of old patients.

Merchant's House Museum
New York, New York

There's a spirit on the loose in this spooky family home.

Victoria and Albert Museum
London, England

Be careful where you rest your head on this giant, haunted bed.

GLOSSARY

ancient (AYN-shunt) very old

coffin (KAW-fin) a long box in which a dead person is buried

corpses (KORPS-iz) bodies of dead people

craftsman (krafts-MEN) a worker whose job requires skills using the hands

legend (LEJ-uhnd) a story handed down from long ago that is often based on some facts but cannot be proven true

morgue (MORG) a place where dead bodies are kept

mummies (MUHM-eez) preserved dead bodies

patients (PAY-shunhnts) people who are getting treatment from a doctor

phantom (FAN-tum) a ghost

punishment (PUHN-ish-muhnt) the penalty for a fault or crime

spirit (SPIHR-it) a ghost

INDEX

READ MORE

Markovics, Joyce. *Deadly Morgues (Tiptoe Into Scary Places).* New York: Bearport (2018).

Merwin, E. *Nightmarish New York (Tiptoe Into Scary Cities).* New York: Bearport (2019).

LEARN MORE ONLINE

1. Go to **www.factsurfer.com**
2. Enter "**Scary Museums**" into the search box.
3. Click on the cover of this book to see a list of websites.

ABOUT THE AUTHOR

Joyce Markovics has written over 100 books for children. She loves old, spooky places and volunteers as a gravestone cleaner in Ossining, New York.